The Art of Art for Children's Books: *A Contemporary Survey*

The Art of Art for Children's Books:
A Contemporary Survey

by Diana Klemin

The Murton Press/Publishers GREENWICH, CONNECTICUT

Library of Congress Cataloging in Publication Data

Klemin, Diana.
   The art of art for children's books.

   Reprint. Originally published: New York:
C.N. Potter, 1966.
   Bibliography: p.
   Includes index.
   1. Illustrated books, Children's. 2. Il-
lustrations of books — 20th century. I. Title.
NC 965.K55 1982   741.64'2'0922   82-80362
ISBN 0-9608042-O-X (pbk.)   AACR2

*Type set in Monotype Bembo by Clarke & Way, Inc., New York. Printed on Glatfelter Vellum
and bound for the publisher by Ray Freiman & Company, Stamford, Connecticut*

To Ethel Klemin
who has lived through
the agony and the pleasure
of the writing and making
of many books

ACKNOWLEDGMENTS

I wish to thank the many artists and editors consulted in the preparation of this book. To Dr. Robert L. Leslie go my thanks for his untiring encouragement and interest from the beginning and even before. I am deeply grateful to Maria Cimino, Richard Jackson, Margaret McElderry, and Maurice Sendak, who discussed and suggested; to Selden Womrath for her courtesy; to Myra Conway, John Hill, and Christopher Pullman at the Yale School of Design for photography; to Michael Horen for assistance in the design of the book; and to Clarkson N. Potter for his enthusiasm.

My thanks are also due to the following publishers and copyright owners for their kind permission to include the illustrations in this collection:

ATHENEUM PUBLISHERS   Milton Glaser: From *Cats and Bats and Things with Wings.* Poems by Conrad Aiken. Illustrations copyright © 1965 by Milton Glaser; Joseph Low: From *Adam's Book of Odd Creatures* by Joseph Low. Copyright © 1962 by Joseph Low; Celestino Piatti: From *The Happy Owls* by Celestino Piatti. Copyright © 1963 by ARTEMIS VERLAG, Zurich, Switzerland. First U.S.A. edition 1964 by ATHENEUM. First published in Great Britain, 1965 by ERNEST BENN, LIMITED; Philip Reed: From *Mother Goose and Nursery Rhymes.* Reprinted by permission of ATHENEUM PUBLISHERS and HAMISH HAMILTON, LTD.; Joseph Schindelman: From *The Great Picture Robbery* by Leon A. Harris. Illustrations copyright © 1963 by Joseph Schindelman; Tomi Ungerer: From *The Three Robbers* by Tomi Ungerer. Copyright © 1962 by Tomi Ungerer. Used by permission of ATHENEUM PUBLISHERS and METHUEN & COMPANY, LTD., London.

THOMAS Y. CROWELL COMPANY   Barbara Cooney: From *A White Heron* by Sarah Orne Jewett. Illustrations copyright © 1963 by Barbara Cooney; Symeon Shimin: From *Listen, Rabbit!* by Aileen Fisher. Text copyright © 1964 by Aileen Fisher. Illustrations copyright © 1964 by Symeon Shimin.

DOUBLEDAY & COMPANY, INC.   Edward Ardizzone: From *The Penny Fiddle* by Robert Graves. Illustrations copyright © 1960 by Edward Ardizzone. Reprinted by permission of DOUBLEDAY & COMPANY, INC. and A. P. WATT & SON; Erik Blegvad: From *Flivver, The Heroic Horse* by Lee Kingman. Illustration copyright © 1958 by Erik Blegvad; Marguerite de Angeli: From *The Goose Girl* by Marguerite de Angeli. Copyright © 1964 by Marguerite de Angeli; Dahlov Ipcar: From *Wild and Tame Animals* by Dahlov Ipcar. Copyright © 1962 by Dahlov Ipcar. Reprinted by permission of DOUBLEDAY & COMPANY, INC. and MCINTOSH & OTIS, INC.; Su Zan Noguchi Swain: From *The Doubleday First Guide to Insects* by Su Zan Noguchi Swain. Copyright © 1964 by Su Zan Noguchi Swain.

GOLDEN PRESS, INC.   Alice and Martin Provensen: From *Shakespeare Ten Great Plays* with commentary by Sir Tyrone Guthrie. Copyright © 1962 by GOLDEN PRESS, INC.; Adrienne Segur: From *The Fairy Tale Book* translated by Marie Ponsot. Copyright © 1958 by GOLDEN PRESS, INC.; Edward Sorel: From *Gwendolyn and the Weathercock* by Nancy Sherman. Copyright © 1963 by GOLDEN PRESS, INC.

GROSSET & DUNLAP, INC.   Gyo Fujikawa: From *A Child's Garden of Verses* by Robert Louis Stevenson. Copyright © 1957 by GROSSET & DUNLAP, INC., publisher.

HARCOURT, BRACE & WORLD, INC.   Joan Walsh Anglund: From *A Friend Is Someone Who Likes You* by Joan Walsh Anglund. Copyright © 1958 by Joan Walsh Anglund. Reproduced by permission of HARCOURT, BRACE

& WORLD, INC. and WILLIAM COLLINS SONS & COMPANY, LTD.; Jacqueline Ayer: From *Nu Dang and His Kite* by Jacqueline Ayer. Copyright © 1959 by Jacqueline Ayer. Reproduced by permission of HARCOURT, BRACE & WORLD, INC. and WILLIAM COLLINS SONS & COMPANY, LTD.; Hans Fischer: From *The Good-for-Nothings* by The Brothers Grimm and Hans Fischer. Reproduced by permission of HARCOURT, BRACE & WORLD, INC. André François: From *Roland* by Nelly Stéphane and André François. Reproduced by permission of HARCOURT, BRACE & WORLD, INC. and BUCHHEIM VERLAG FELDAFING; Antonio Frasconi from *See and Say* by Antonio Frasconi. Copyright © 1955 by Antonio Frasconi; Irene Haas from *A Little House of Your Own* by Beatrice Schenk de Regniers and Irene Haas. Illustrations copyright © 1954 by Irene Haas. Reproduced by permission of HARCOURT, BRACE & WORLD, INC. and WILLIAM COLLINS SONS & COMPANY, LTD.; Nicolas [Mordvinoff]: From *Finders Keepers* by William Lipkind and Nicolas [Mordvinoff]. Copyright © 1951 by William Lipkind and Nicolas [Mordvinoff]. Reproduced by permission of HARCOURT, BRACE & WORLD, INC. and THE WORLD'S WORK, LTD.; Leona Pierce: From *Who Likes the Sun?* by Beatrice Schenk de Regniers and Leona Pierce. Illustrations copyright © 1961 by Leona Pierce. Reproduced by permission of HARCOURT, BRACE & WORLD, INC. and WILLIAM COLLINS SONS & COMPANY, LTD.; Paul Rand: From *I Know a Lot of Things* by Ann and Paul Rand. Copyright © 1956 by Ann and Paul Rand. Reproduced by permission of HARCOURT, BRACE & WORLD, INC. and WILLIAM COLLINS SONS & COMPANY, LTD.; Bill Sokol: From *A Child's Book of Dreams* by Beatrice Schenk de Regniers and Bill Sokol. Illustrations copyright © 1957 by William Sokol. Reproduced by permission of HARCOURT, BRACE & WORLD, INC. and Beatrice Schenk de Regniers; Jerome Snyder: From *One Day in Aztec Mexico* by G. B. Kirtland. Illustrations copyright © 1963 by Jerome Snyder.

HARPER & ROW, PUBLISHERS Margaret Bloy Graham: From *The Plant Sitter* by Gene Zion with pictures by Margaret Bloy Graham. Pictures copyright © 1959 by Margaret Bloy Graham. Reproduced by permission of HARPER & ROW, PUBLISHERS and THE BODLEY HEAD, LTD.; Maurice Sendak: From *Mr. Rabbit and the Lovely Present* by Charlotte Zolotow. Copyright © 1962 by Maurice Sendak; Marc Simont: From *The Happy Day* by Ruth Krauss, pictures by Marc Simont. Pictures copyright © 1949 by Marc Simont; Garth Williams: From *Charlotte's Web* by E. B. White. Reproduced by permission of HARPER & ROW, PUBLISHERS and HAMISH HAMILTON, LTD.

HOLT, RINEHART AND WINSTON, INC. Maurice Sendak: From *The Griffin and the Minor Canon* by Frank R. Stockton. Illustrations copyright © 1963 by Maurice Sendak; Susanne Suba: From *A Rocket in My Pocket* compiled by Carl Withers. Copyright © 1948 by Carl Withers; William Wondriska: From *Which Way to the Zoo?* by William Wondriska. Copyright © 1961 by William Wondriska.

HOUGHTON MIFFLIN COMPANY Lynd Ward: From *The Biggest Bear* by Lynd Ward. Copyright © 1952 by Lynd Ward.

INSEL-VERLAG Fritz Kredel: From *Grimm's Fairy Tales* with woodcuts by Fritz Kredel.

ALFRED A. KNOPF, INC. Marvin Bileck: From *Nobody's Birthday* written by Anne Colver. Copyright © 1961 by Anne Colver and Marvin Bileck; Nancy Ekholm Burkert: From *James and the Giant Peach* by Roald Dahl. Copyright © 1961 by Roald Dahl; Warren Chappell: From *They Say Stories* written and illustrated by Warren Chappell. Copyright © 1960 by Warren Chappell; Roger Duvoisin: From *Petunia Takes a Trip* written and illustrated by Roger Duvoisin. Copyright © 1953. Reproduced by permission of ALFRED A. KNOPF, INC. and THE BODLEY HEAD, LTD.; Beni Montresor: From *The Witches of Venice* written and illustrated by Beni Montresor. Copyright © 1963 by Beni Montresor. Reproduced by permission of ALFRED A. KNOPF, INC. and ASHLEY FAMOUS AGENCY, INC.; Feodor Rojankovsky: From *The Whirly Bird* by Dimitry Varley. Copyright © 1961 by Dimitry Varley and Feodor Rojankovsky.

J. B. LIPPINCOTT COMPANY Tasha Tudor: From *The Secret Garden* by Frances Hodgson Burnett. Copyright © 1911 by F. H. Burnett. Copyright © renewal 1938 by Verity Constance Burnett. Illustrations copyright © 1962 by J. B. LIPPINCOTT COMPANY.

CONTENTS

The Storytellers

The concepts that lie behind the illustrated book for children should be studied and examined and it is with this topic that I am concerned. Fortunately for children, editors believe that the illustrated book is a necessity. Look back at the acceptance of *Alice's Adventures in Wonderland* and follow the history of its many editions, and you will find that it always had illustrations, usually by Tenniel. Authors depend upon the artist's contribution to establish their tale, but above all, artists themselves have felt the need to draw for children, who are a most appreciative audience. They have found in these assignments considerable freedom to experiment with the printed medium as an art form and, in addition, an opportunity for personal involvement and expression. As a result, the children's book is now the focus of immense graphic excitement and activity.

The present renaissance of children's book illustration began with the picture book in the late nineteen twenties. At that time the artist could paint or draw with little editorial direction, and as offset printing gradually superseded letterpress, the artist was no longer confined even by the mechanical limitations of a letterpress type page. He could "bleed" his illustrations by drawing or painting to the extreme edges of the book page, and he could place type as freely as he did the drawings outside the traditional text areas. He grew to be responsible for the *mise en pages*, and a book became an entirety stamped with his individuality. Gradually, good book illustration reached most juvenile books, and today the creativity is so alive and appropriate that the art is worthy of adult interest. Turn to *Wuthering Heights* forcefully illustrated by Bernarda Bryson or *The Aeneid for Boys and Girls* with its pertinent episodes illustrated by Eugene Karlin. Here the artists have not talked down to the readers and have achieved a contribution worthy of these classics.

Are illustrations directed toward children or adults? Does it matter? How is this magical and voluminous array of work to be sorted and judged?

I gathered the work of contemporary masters, those artists who have illustrated children's books for a decade or more, and also the newcomers, who in a short time have evolved a mature style. In this way I could select the outstanding work of those who have really contributed, given intensely of themselves, and who are the pacesetters who inspire many imitators. These are the creative persons who are masters of technique, can grasp the meaning of a book, are devoted to the art of illustration, and understand its relation to the story. They have visualization, imagination, and inner fire to make a meaningful graphic statement and to integrate it with the text until story and illustration are one. I have purposely left out those dexterous in the fine arts like Ben Shahn, Leonard Baskin, and others who can turn their hand to a children's book as readily as they can paint, sculpt, or draw.

The artist is equally an inspirer with the author in the tradition of children's book illustration. The art and text blend in such perfect harmony that a child remembers the illustrations as an integral part of a story. *Stuart Little* appears to the child to belong as much to E. B. White as to Garth Williams, and *Alice's Adventures in Wonderland* is fully the work of Lewis Carroll and John Tenniel. The late E. McKnight Kauffer stressed this magnificently at the International Book Illustration show* in New York City when he said he saw no reason why an illustrator should be rushed to illustrate a book. If W. H. Hudson took twenty years to write *Green Mansions*, then the artist should be allowed that length of time for his graphic contribution. It is this tradition of the creative storytelling technique that is my prime concern. It is the work of the artists, the masters of the book craft who believe that the function of illustration is the creation and development of characters and the portrayal of the scenes necessary in mood or action to bring the story to completion. Each drawing, each painting contributes another image, adds a new dimension. The artists achieve such an intense relationship with the story that a child participates in it by identifying himself with the characters, places, and scenes of the tale. Children demand a faithful interpretation of the text, and want representational drawing and design of the subject. Hands must have all the right fingers, and the number of persons, animals, or objects mentioned must be pictured in the color as described. Above all, the artists want to submerge themselves in the story so that the end result is a collaboration with the author so as to present the tale the way they think children would like to experience it. They want to depict the wicked, the unpleasant, the terrifying moment along with the festive and glorious ones, and to bring out the brave and dauntless character of the hero. Today Edward Ardizzone, Roger Duvoisin, Edy Legrand, Nicolas [Mordvinoff], and Maurice Sendak illustrate with the brilliance, scope, and spirit of the late Edmund Dulac, Howard Pyle, Arthur Rackham, and N. C. Wyeth.

Then there are those artists who approach a book from a more personal and poetic point of view. Their technique is to illuminate the text. The visual im-

---

International Book Illustration, 1935–1945, show, assembled by the American Institute of Graphic Arts, took place from October 1st to 31st in 1946 at the Morgan Library.

pression is one of charm, beauty, and mood. Sometimes they write their own story or they find a gentle tale or a collection of poetry and set the scene for it. Look at the work of Jacqueline Ayer, Barbara Cooney, Irene Haas, Adrienne Adams, and Beni Montresor to see the effect they create by their scenes and decoration. These become a backdrop for the author's words. The keen observation of and concern for minute detail in dress, settings, and landscapes convey a feeling of characterization and a suggestion of action in storytelling. They also capture a living picture of a child's world of play and make-believe.

Another facet of the children's book is those imaginary works of morals and aphorisms. Part of their intent is to help the adult recapture and enjoy the child's world of make-believe and fantasy. The illustrations and graphics of Joan Walsh Anglund, Edward Sorel, Joseph Low, and Antonio Frasconi have a childhood nostalgia, an ironic twist, and whimsy. Yet the vividness, excitement, and vitality of the graphic expression the artist generates can also be enjoyed by a child at his own level. The type is equally well handled and the design of each book is exceptional and appropriate.

Other artists are masters of collage and abstraction. They play humorously with color and form, and transform the commonplace into something extraordinary or memorable. More stylists than storytellers, they entertain the youngest children with effects as magic as kaleidoscopes, and introduce them to the beautiful aesthetic experience of a book. An important contribution of these artists is the reawakening of adults to the exquisite perfection in the graphic arts and to the delights of abstractions.

The specialists I refer to are those artists who have been drawn to the biological or physical sciences and who, by their curiosity and diligence, have become naturalists in their own right. They not only illustrate but create and write with lucidity and imagination reference books that appeal to both children and adults. Only a small group is represented here, with a suggestion to explore further for others dedicated to this form of art.

In the pages that follow, notice how differently each artist communicates to the child and to the adult. I hope the selection arouses curiosity and desire to obtain the actual books for further study. No reproduction of a single page or double-spread can capture the beauty, pleasure, and excitement of the original graphic delight of a book. Sometimes I had to substitute for the intricate and flamboyantly colored drawing a simpler one that would have meaning in black-and-white reproduction. Since many of the artists have illustrated dozens of magnificent books, limiting the choice to one example was often difficult and did not always represent the wide scope of their talents. Also the grouping of the artists into suggested categories must be considered flexible and merely a starting point for discussion, as these creative people continually change, experiment, and grow. Because of space limitations many other fine artists are not included.

To quote Edward Johnson, "Nothing is reproduced. Something different is produced."* Thus I have not discussed preparation of artwork or technical reproduction processes in detail. Each book selected is evidence of excellent draftsmanship by experts who have studied and absorbed techniques and chosen their preference for art preparation. Instead I have just given a sparse suggestion of what is to be seen in the original book, and limited my descriptions to basic categories—line, pencil or wash drawings, woodcut, and lithograph. "Color separation" means that the base drawing was on one board and the color was applied on separate and successive overlays. "Watercolor" refers to full color painting whether in tempera or gouache. Remember that the chance of seeing the original art is slight. It is the printed book that is examined and judged. Therefore the dynamics of book illustration can readily be studied from black-and-white reproductions.

In the limited color section I have selected three storytellers, Edward Ardizzone, Edy Legrand, and Symeon Shimin, who actually compose in color, and one storyteller, Nancy Ekholm Burkert, who in this case composes in black and white and adds color afterward. The final result is equally charming. Leonard Weisgard is an example of the decorative, poetic painter, while Leo Lionni and Celestino Piatti, whose works depend upon color and do not successfully translate into black-and-white reproduction, brilliantly represent collage and abstraction.

*Lynton Lamb, *Drawing for Illustration*, London, 1962, p. 3.

The Storytellers

EDWARD ARDIZZONE

ERIK BLEGVAD

VLADIMIR BOBRI

MARCIA BROWN

NANCY EKHOLM BURKERT *(see color section)*

BERNARDA BRYSON

WARREN CHAPPELL

WILLIAM PÈNE duBOIS

ROGER DUVOISIN

MARIE HALL ETS

HANS FISCHER

GYO FUJIKAWA

MARGARET BLOY GRAHAM

ROBIN JACQUES

EUGENE KARLIN

FRITZ KREDEL

EDY LEGRAND *(see color section)*

NICOLAS [MORDVINOFF]

SEONG MOY

EVALINE NESS

HENRY C. PITZ

PHILIP REED

FEODOR ROJANKOVSKY

JOSEPH SCHINDELMAN

ADRIENNE SEGUR

MAURICE SENDAK

SYMEON SHIMIN

MARC SIMONT

LAWRENCE BEALL SMITH

JEROME SNYDER

TASHA TUDOR

LYND WARD

GARTH WILLIAMS

EDWARD ARDIZZONE
The Penny Fiddle,
line in color separation,
6⅛ × 9¼ inches

This master illustrator is a
storyteller who thoroughly
understands a child's desire
to identify himself with the
hero of the tale or poem,
and sets out to have the
child do this willingly.
Here playing make-believe
the children really walk as
king and queen. At times
they take a more adven-
turous part as in the watercolor example from the
artist's favorite, *Little Tim
and the Brave Sea Captain*.
Ardizzone has a natural
fondness for children, and
his love of detail gives
warmth to scenes memo-
rable in beauty, mood, and
action.

Henry and Mary

Henry was a young king,
  Mary was his queen;
He gave her a snowdrop
  On a stalk of green.

Then all for his kindness
  And all for his care
She gave him a new-laid egg
  In the garden there.

'Love, can you sing?'
                      'I canne
  'Or tell a tale?'
'   'Not one
'Then let us play at queen and
  As down the garden walks

g.'

ow.'

go.'

"Can't say as I'm sorry," sputtered Captain Truesdale. "Ever since that horse came to Snuggler's Cove our kids have gone crazy. When I saw them pretending an old rowboat was a stagecoach, it got me right mad."

"I been ambushed tw rescued by the Lone S young Herbert Armitag sea legs, where I been br the Coast Guard."

"That horse is a bad i Armitage. "Well, this da

and held up once, and
...ger three times," said
Kind of gets me in my
...ht up to get rescued by

...ence," said old Herbert
...ill see the last of him!"

ERIK BLEGVAD
Flivver, the Heroic Horse,
line drawings, 6⅛ × 9¼ inches

No episode is too small for Blegvad to
pause and make it a story in pictures with
his sly humor and gentle manner. He tucks
the drawings into the text, and they illuminate the whole scene as if he had been
sketching while looking over the author's
shoulder. Who else could fill such a scene
as this one with the fishermen relaxed and
chatting, the children at play in their world,
and the cat basking in the sun? Early in the
story, when Flivver, the horse, is having
his portrait painted, Blegvad has the imagination and technique to draw the horse
sitting on the sofa in a most natural manner.
When this artist does use color, he adds it
fetchingly in delicate and bright tints of
watercolor.

VLADIMIR BOBRI *The March Wind*, wash in separation and watercolor, 7¼ × 9 inches

Bobri is a stylist. Here is his blending of realism with abstraction. Because he has mischief, exuberance, and imagination, a fantasy comes alive and a little boy is a convincing hero in his escapades with the March wind. Even the change from flamboyant to somber in the handling of color reflects the various moods of the story. The entire effect is one of enjoyment, for Bobri has made his art a contribution to the author's tale.

BERNARDA BRYSON *Wuthering Heights,*
line and watercolor, 5⅞ × 8⅞ inches

This haunting scene catches the sinister, brooding mood of all of *Wuthering Heights*. Bernarda Bryson imagined it just this way when she was a young girl, and kept this concept alive in her memory for many years. The intensity and passion of her fine drawing with its eerie quality, faded color, and patterns and rhythms of the wind lead one right into the story, and give much to ponder about.

46 They spent the whole night in weaving a net out of the pliant willow bark and stout reeds, and it was large and strong. On it Elisa lay down, and when the sun came up and the brothers changed into wild swans, they gripped the net in their beaks and flew high up towards the clouds, with their dear sister, who was still asleep. The sunbeams fell hotly on her face, so one of the swans flew above her head, that his broad wings might shade her.

MARCIA BROWN *The Wild Swans,*
wash drawing in color separation, 7¼ × 10 inches

Tenderly in gentle colors these illustrations make the drama of a fairy tale believable. Knowing this story can be read aloud, the observant Marcia

They were far from land when Elisa awoke. She thought she was still dreaming, so strange it seemed to her to be borne over the sea, high through the air. At her side lay a branch with beautiful ripe berries on it, and a bundle of sweet-tasting roots. Her youngest brother had gathered them and laid them by her; and she smiled gratefully at him, for she knew it was he who was flying straight over her head and shading her with his wings.

47

Brown follows every word with a wealth of pictures about the beautiful heroine, Elisa. Specifically, as the text tells, the artist draws Elisa with berries and roots at her side and being carried in a net over a sparkling sea by the eleven swans. One sees the expanse of water and feels the ardor of the task performed with devotion.

The banker bowed; the butcher and the baker bowed; everyone bowed.

Even Sam Small bowed, though not because he expected any favor. Sam was only a tenant farmer, who lived with his daughter,

26

WARREN CHAPPELL *They Say Stories*,
line and watercolor, 5⅝ × 8¼ inches

The illustrations have a timeless quality that matches these folk tales, and as one reads, all comes to life. Here is the essence of the story in this single

Buttercup, in the meanest cabin on the poorest
piece of land in all the Goldfleece acres. He
did not mind the fact that the squire ignored
him, except when the rent was due, but he was
saddened by the way Sunflower treated his dear
little Buttercup.

27

scene and in velvety-toned color. The carriage rolls by with the haughty
while the solid, subservient citizenry looks on. Warren Chappell, equally
an artist, book designer, and typographer, concerns himself with sound
draftsmanship and historical groundwork as well as the exact placement of
each illustration throughout the book.

WILLIAM PÈNE DuBOIS
Lion,
line in color separation, 7⅝ × 10 inches

The artist plans this world of fantasy with such logic and ease that one could participate in this very scene by flying one of his kites. Later on, as characters and animals appear individually, each has a fetching personality. There is harmony between the story and the pictures, and there is always a delightful surprise on the next page. William Pène duBois seems to have opened a luscious box of colors and used them sparingly and with care at the right time.

7

Long, long ago, high up in the sky, way above the clouds, there was a white and silver

ROGER DUVOISIN *Petunia Takes a Trip*, line in color separation, 8 × 10 inches

The next day, the policeman and his wife took Petunia to a railroad station so big it would have enclosed a mountain. They kissed Petunia and Petunia waved to them when the train started off.

"Come and visit me in the country," she cried to her kind friends.

The scope, the variety, and the change of pace of the drawings are fantastic in storytelling about this lovable goose in a busy, human world. Each double-spread in clean line or clear color has two distinct and busy adventures that are completely self-contained. Duvoisin can picture contagious humor with seemingly little effort. With equal zest Paul Galdone illustrates in this adventurous way for *Anatole*, the story of a mouse.

From her seat by the train window, Petunia watched the green fields, the SMALL houses, the SMALL streams, as they glided by and she felt more and more like a real-size goose again. She was happy.

"It's good to go home," she said to herself.

MARIE HALL ETS *Nine Days to Christmas,*
pencil in color separation, 7⅝ × 11 inches

The very young will explore again and again these pictures where solid
children are busy enjoying daily activities. The more they look, the more
there is to find in this gentle story drawn in festive colors. Marie Hall Ets
has that homespun touch of Wanda Gág, and presents her little heroine
from a child's viewpoint. Another artist, Richard Scarry, in his *Busy, Busy
World* also handles a painting story within a story with colorful humor.

The next day, as on every other day, Ceci's big brother, Salvador,
left her at the kindergarten gate on his way to school. And as on every
day Ceci watered the flowers in the big garden, and danced in a circle,
and painted pictures. But at noon, just before it was time for the

8

children to run to the gate to see who was waiting for them, Ceci's teacher called her group together under the pepper tree and gave each child a pretty candy and said good-by. For, unlike other days, today was the last day of school.

Early in the morning, before it was quite light and when nobody was stirring in the inn, Chanticleer woke his wife.

HANS FISCHER   *The Good-for-Nothings,*
line in color separation, 11¾ × 7 inches

This is how a child would like to draw a picture book. Hans
Fischer has taken a handful of colors, and assigned a different
one to each animal character and object. Chanticleer and his
wife sport daring blue feathers as they appear in action, and
every phrase of the text has decided imaginative touches by the
artist. The color sparkles against the white background—
except for a surprise scene done in the black of night—and the
drawings are free in style, the design flowing and natural
throughout. As only a master illustrator could make this
happen, it is no wonder Hans Fischer has had a great influence
on other artists.

He fetched the egg they had given to the landlord. They pecked a hole in it, ate it up, and threw the shell into the fireplace.

GYO FUJIKAWA *A Child's Garden of Verses,*
line and watercolor, 8½ × 12 inches

For little children the joy is to find little things in pictures. Observant, loving, humorous, Gyo Fujikawa lets her imagination play with this theme in delicate colors with an exquisite touch. There is also a healthy influence from Disneyland, more evident in her *The Night Before Christmas* and *Babies.*

My Ship and I

O it's I that am the captain of a tidy little ship,
    Of a ship that goes a-sailing on the pond;
And my ship it keeps a-turning all around and all about;
But when I'm a little older, I shall find the secret out
    How to send my vessel sailing on beyond.

For I mean to grow as little as the dolly at the helm,
    And the dolly I intend to come alive;
And with him beside to help me, it's a-sailing I shall go,
It's a-sailing on the water, when the jolly breezes blow
    And the vessel goes a divie-divie-dive.

70

O it's then you'll see me sailing through the rushes and the reeds,
    And you'll hear the water singing at the prow;
For beside the dolly sailor, I'm to voyage and explore,
To land upon the island where no dolly was before,
    And to fire the penny cannon in the bow.

Even the bathroom was full of plants.

Having a bath was like swimming in a little lake

in the middle of a beautiful forest.

MARGARET BLOY GRAHAM *The Plant Sitter*,
line in color separation, 8 × 10⅞ inches

A helpful and real little boy becomes absorbed in his hobby of plant-sitting.
In her charming, comic style and with an imaginative use of shades of green,

But one night Tommy almost fell asleep in the tub.
Plant sitting was hard work and he was tired.
"You'd better go to bed, dear," said his mother.
"You've got to get up early and water those plants."

the artist fills each episode with mischief and nonsense. Margaret Bloy
Graham's contribution is a major one because she adds busy little touches
to the text and gives a sense of the continuity of daily life. She introduces
Tommy's cat and dog, and entwines their doings in his story. Children will
follow these adventures with high hopes that they can have more of them.

ghty Days

noke of his pipe, a series
ompliment to the audi-
ed candles, which he ex-
I his lips, and relit again
us juggling. Another re-
ations with a spinning-
seemed to be animated
rminable whirling. They
res, wires and even hairs
d around on the edges of
s, dispersed into all the
l effects by the combina-
The jugglers tossed them
cks with wooden battle-
they put them into their
ing as before.

ishing performances of
rning on ladders, poles,
wonderful precision.
e exhibition of the Long
yet a stranger.

company, under the di-
Attired after the fashion
heir shoulders a splendid
distinguished them was
to their faces, and the
ese noses were made of
en ten feet long, some
ed and some having im-
these appendages, fixed
performed their gymnas-

ROBIN JACQUES   *Around the World in Eighty Days*, line and watercolor, 5½ × 8¼ inches

Literal and lively, this fastidious draftsman delights in giving his characters their place in a story with elegant
details of clothes, furniture, and settings. Robin Jacques always considers the effect of reproduction upon a
drawing, and designs his scenes to fill the unwieldy proportions of a book page. He is personally sympathetic
to nineteenth-century England, and his watercolors have the soft, rich quality reminiscent of the Victorian
color printing done from wood blocks.

nius, and other fine
to the boy: "Take
was once Hector's
the very image of
so cruelly. Your ey
and indeed, if he w
age as you." Then
you," he said, "who
found your rest. Yo
to seek this land of
as we follow it. You
eyes. Farewell, and
of Italy, there shall
and between your

After this they s
they drew their shi
but at midnight th
nurus, roused himse
a note of the weath
were bright, the G
Orion, with his be
"These are signs of
time." So he blew
starting. And all the
Through the darkn
ing was growing rec
there was a land w
shore lying low. Th
is the land of Italy

"He was a horrible cre
blind. He came down

EUGENE KARLIN   *The Aeneid for Boys and Girls*, line drawings, 5⅞ × 8⅞ inches

Eugene Karlin's line flows along gracefully and with a purpose. Everything the artist touches radiates beauty and enchantment, and when he uses color, he wafts it lightly in pastel shafts. This vivid drawing of Cyclops has a mural quality, neoclassic in form and legendary in content.

FRITZ KREDEL *Grimm's Fairy Tales*, woodcuts and watercolor, 6 × 9 inches

A true and natural illustrator, Fritz Kredel is sensitive to the needs of a story, and can be humorous, witty, or poetic. He depicts character, and adds the little touches that decorate a scene. Here he gives a terrifying moment from "The King's Son Who Feared Nothing" in a style that combines an uncluttered line with muted color.

SEONG MOY *Uncle Remus, His Songs and His Sayings*, woodcuts, 8 × 9½ inches

Seong Moy combines a bold abstract expressionism with an extraordinary storytelling realism in the medium of the woodcut. Here he suggests in a pattern of solid round stones a country well and the movement of Brer Rabbit's bucket to the top while Brer Fox's falls. His animal characters outwit each other with spirit and a lively folk humor that is far different from the original, splendid A. B. Frost drawings for this classic, although Seong Moy's are equally meaningful in interpretation.

NICOLAS [MORDVINOFF]   *Finders Keepers,*
line in color separation, 8¼ × 10⅞ inches

The graphics of Nicolas are as inventive and expressive in storytelling as the

"Mr. Hairtrimmer," said Nap, "Winkle and I found a bone. Whose should it be, his or mine? I saw it first."

"But I touched it first," said Winkle.

"Just let me trim your hair a bit to try my tools and I'll see what I can do," said the barber.

writing of Will Lipkind. Nicolas thinks in line enforced with blazing color as he clearly plans every turn of the tale. What happiness, disgust, ferocity, pride, and contentment are pictured in the faces of the rascals, Nap and Winkle, in their many hilarious adventures.

He went at Winkle's hair with his scissors, clipping and snipping, while Nap looked on and smiled.

Then Nap had his hair cut, while Winkle looked on and smiled.

However, the last day of the eleventh month he takes

her to a room she'd never set eyes on before.

There was nothing in it but a spinning wheel

and a stool. And says he, "Now, my dear,

here you'll be shut in tomorrow with

some victuals and some flax, and if

you haven't spun five skeins by

the night, your head'll go off."

And away he went about

his business.

Well, she was that frightened, she'd

always been such a gatless girl, that she

didn't so much as know how to spin, and what

was she to do tomorrow with no one to come

nigh her to help her? She sat down on the stool and

LAW, HOW SHE DID CRY!

EVALINE NESS
Tom Tit Tot,
woodcuts in color
separation, 8 × 10 inches

The artist accomplishes in
wood and color what
others do with brush or
pen. This lively, short tale
gives Evaline Ness great
scope of selectivity of scene
and character portrayal.
Like a sincere craftsman,
she works out a full and
hearty picture book, and
uses the text as a vital part
of each composition.

HENRY C. PITZ *King Arthur and His Knights,*
line and watercolor, 5½ × 8¼ inches

In the illustrating tradition of Howard Pyle and N. C. Wyeth, this artist,
Henry C. Pitz, re-creates an era. His interest is not in intimate character studies,

but he provides real action in his drawings and soft watercolors. For this book he fills his scenes with knights who actually breathe inside their armor while their horses charge ahead. He can catch the mood of a gentle damsel awaiting the return of a warrior, or the regal King Arthur presiding at court.

Rub-a-dub-dub!
Three men in a tub;
And who do you think they be?
The butcher, the baker
The candle-stick maker;
Turn 'em out knaves all three!

8

PHILIP REED   *Mother Goose and Nursery Rhymes*,
wood engravings in color separation, 7¾ × 10¾ inches

The excitement of this endearingly old-fashioned edition of *Mother Goose*
lies in Philip Reed's ability to choose a lively moment and to set it profusely

Hickory, dickory, dock,
The mouse ran up the clock.
The clock struck one,
The mouse ran down,
Hickory, dickory, dock.

Little Tommy Tittlemouse
Lived in a little house;
He caught fishes
In other men's ditches.

9

in six colors against a spacious white background. It is apparent this illustrator is an enthusiast of eighteenth-century English children's books, those published by John Newbery and those conceived by Thomas Bewick. He effects a pastiche in the tradition and, as his own typographer, wood engraver, and printer, delights in the making of a complete and sturdy book.

FEODOR ROJANKOVSKY *The Whirly Bird*,
pencil in color separation, 8 × 10 inches

The warm and sensitive Feodor Rojankovsky absorbs every word of a story
until he becomes a part of it. Then he plans his compositions to entice and surprise
as in these facing pages where he handles three exciting moments of emotion

"What can I do? Is there no one to help me?" the robin cried
to himself, and closed his eyes. At that very moment Jenny came
running from the house, her shiny yellow braids flying. She had
seen it all from the window and hoped she would not be too late.
"Shoo!" she screamed.

and action. He respects his characters as real people and knows their habits and manners. His young animals and birds with their trusting innocence ask to be held, stroked, and talked to. Expertly in color separation he builds up shape and form with light and shadow whether in two colors or in the complete palette of four, and the effect is of natural patterns and true, gay color.

The Cat jumped down, looked at Jenny with angry eyes, and then, disappointed and still hungry, quickly slunk away. There is no animal as strong as Jenny, thought the robin gratefully. He even let her stroke his head, though he was still so scared he sat down on his tail.

There are no kings of France these days, so the rooms of the Louvre are filled with paintings and statues and other old things that people come to see. This is fine with Maurice, except that he does not really enjoy the people. Some of them do not like mice.

JOSEPH SCHINDELMAN *The Great Picture Robbery*,
line in color separation, 8¼ × 7¼ inches

As Joseph Schindelman draws each page, he mingles two viewpoints clearly, that of Maurice, the tender mouse hero, who has a lively time in the Louvre where the visitors and even the statues watch him furtively. Then there is the other, the artist's making the museum's interior an experience of endless exploration into the treasures of the past. With touches of color he can sketch the Winged Victory in all her aura or equally well the mouse nibbling a delectable pastry.

ADRIENNE SEGUR *The Fairy Tale Book,*
line in color separation and watercolor, 9½ × 12¾ inches

Adrienne Segur paints each illustration like a tapestry, magnificent in story, color, and texture.
With characters whose faces resemble delicate porcelain, and whose companions are down-
feathered birds and silken animals, she brings forth all the emotion and beauty that enchant children
to become part of the world of make-believe. Her line drawings take the form of embroidery
in intricate, fascinating patterns.

Griffin. "Go down to the very tail of the class; and if you are not at the head in two days, I shall know the reason why."

The next afternoon this boy was Number One.

It was astonishing how much these children now learned of what they had been studying. It was as if they had been educated over again. The Griffin used no severity toward them, but there was a look about him which made them unwilling to go to bed until they were sure they knew their lessons for the next day.

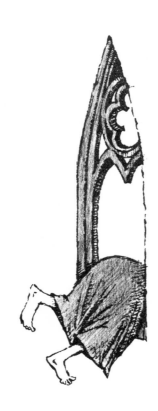

The Griffin now thought that he ought to visit the sick and the poor; and he began to go about the town for this purpose. The effect upon the sick was miraculous. All, except those who were very ill indeed, jumped from their beds when they heard he was coming, and declared themselves quite well. To those who could not get up, he gave herbs and roots, which none of them had ever before thought of as medicines, but which the Griffin had seen used in various parts of the world; and most of them

MAURICE SENDAK   *The Griffin and the Minor Canon*,   line in color separation, 7½ × 8 inches

Maurice Sendak does not merely draw pictures of the author's words. It is in a true sense of "collaboration" that he adds new images and dimensions and makes each scene another step in the development of the story. Who but Sendak could depict this fantastic and thoroughly enjoyable experience of a firm, strong-willed, and well-meaning Griffin? With every book this artist sets out to illustrate, he is as excited by the *mise en pages* as he is with interpretation of character and atmosphere and the interplay of color. This gift of creation is to be studied in many of his other books like *Little Bear*, *The Nutshell Library*, *Where the Wild Things Are*, and *Sarah's Room*.

SYMEON SHIMIN   *One Small Blue Bead*, wash in color separation, 8 × 10 inches

Symeon Shimin has the vision and the skill to make a picture book *tout d'une pièce* and the understanding to make it believable. He creates an imaginative era of early man, paints a powerful story with simplicity, and sustains a wondrous mood in glowing color. The illustrations change pace dramatically from quiet landscapes to group activities and candid character studies of the children.

"The entire road has been greased with bacon rinds. There can be nothing more exquisite."

Now they came into the festive hall. On the right hand stood all the little lady mice. And they whispered and giggled as if they were making fun of each other. On the left stood all the gentlemen mice, stroking their whiskers with their forepaws. And in the center of the hall the bridegroom and bride were standing in a hollow cheese rind, kissing each other terribly before all the guests. For this was the betrothal, and the marriage was to follow immediately.

More and more strangers kept flocking in. One mouse nearly trod another to death. The happy couple had stationed themselves in the doorway, so that one could neither come in nor go out. Like the passage, the room had been greased with bacon rinds, and that was the entire banquet. But for dessert a pea was produced. In it a mouse, belonging to the

LAWRENCE BEALL SMITH *Andersen's Fairy Tales*, wash and watercolor, 5⅞ × 8⅞ inches

A romantic portraitist gives children a sense of participation in this story with a single drawing that arouses their imagination. If Hjalmar, the boy, were to awaken suddenly, Ole Shut-Eye would be alive and so would the mouse. Lawrence Beall Smith's watercolors have a dreamy softness that sustains the mood.

MARC SIMONT *The Happy Day*, pencil in color separation, 8⅝ × 11⅝ inches

Here is a beautiful picture book that is a storytelling in contrasts. Working in gradations of black and white, Marc Simont shows squirrels, bears, groundhogs, snails, and field mice simultaneously in their winter habitats where they sleep, sniff, and run as in real life. He designs each page in a

They cry, "Oh!
A flower is growing in the snow."

rhythm of patterns that is a pleasure to look at, and never forgets to build surprise and excitement to the end which he celebrates with a flash of color. *The Happy Day* is a friendly book. Now turn to *The Lovely Summer* and *The Trail-Driving Rooster* and explore the artist's innate comic gift where with a single stroke he can change an animal's scowl to a smile.

but before she had
l breathless that she
because she had al-
h a little laugh of
swaying on a long
greeted her with a
lt something heavy
d when she saw the

y," she said. "You
believe you know!"
y on to the top of
lovely trill, merely
dorably lovely as a
always doing it.
Magic in her Ayah's
almost at that mo-

own the walk, and
ng enough to wave
a strong enough to
ging from the wall.
ly the gust of wind
suddenly still she
his she did because
b which had been
e knob of a door.
n to pull and push
all was a loose and
er wood and iron.
shake a little in her
ing and twittering
ere as excited as she
square and made of

TASHA TUDOR   *The Secret Garden*, pencil and watercolor, 6⅜ × 8⅜ inches

This scene, nostalgic of nineteenth-century illustration, is a wistful study of the precise moment
in the story. Mellow and cheerful, Tasha Tudor carries on in the tradition of Walter Crane, Kate
Greenaway, and Reginald Birch. Her children and animals are always lovely, her color is without
affectation, and her pencil drawings have the same tonal values.

EDWARD ARDIZZONE *Little Tim and the Brave Sea Captain*,
line and watercolor, 7½ × 10 inches

The first edition of this book was without text, and the watercolors dramatically told the story of little Tim. This meaningful kind of realistic storytelling in pictures follows the fine English tradition of Walter Crane and Randolph Caldecott. Ardizzone always draws with a firm line to which he adds a soft wash in one color as in *The Penny Fiddle* or combines it with complete color as in *Little Tim and the Brave Sea Captain*. Enjoyably he catches every facet of emotion and personality, sets the flavor of a scene, and records the elements at sea. He does not hesitate to borrow from the "comics" the balloon inserts for dialogue, for his goal is always to delight the child.

NANCY EKHOLM BURKERT   *James and the Giant Peach*, line in color separation, 7 × 10 inches

The charm of Nancy Ekholm Burkert's drawings lies in the reminiscence of a bygone era of children's books. She listens to every word of a story. Then, intuitively, she knows where to place the drawings, and when to surprise in complete color. In this magic scene the color heightens the effect of the giant peach as if it were a balloon while the thin red border suggests the tipped-in watercolor of yesteryear.

EDY LEGRAND   "The Bremen Town Musicians,"
watercolor, 5½ × 8¼ inches

Edy Legrand can state instantly in line and in color what he perceives. A scene
is created. Alive and brazen, the characters take their part in it. This is the
culmination of storytelling in illustration and the reason why artists turn to
Edy Legrand for inspiration and study.

CELESTINO PIATTI *The Happy Owls,*
watercolor, 11¾ × 8¼ inches

Dedicated to the art of the poster, Piatti turns his
dazzling talent to children's books. His illustrations can
stand alone as an expression of color and form, the
essence of near abstraction, for they offer much to
muse about. Through their sequence they cast a powerful illusion of storytelling, not by deep character study
or action scenes, but by feeding the imagination and
making an event climactic and important. At last
these winsome owls are happy and together and, if
one ponders long enough, their eyes sparkle and blink.
The typography is bold and simple throughout and
the *mise en pages* is entirely controlled by Piatti as in
his *Animal ABC* where the paintings are tender and
saucy and are filled with comic delight.

"Listen, rabbit!"
I laughed and cried,
feeling all shiny
and warm inside.
"What a wonderful
secret surprise I've spied,
what a wonderful secret
for you to hide."

I hadn't a pony
or pup
to pet,

I hadn't a rabbit
exactly, yet,

But I
had a nest
like a fur-lined cup

And *five baby rabbits*
to watch grow up!

SYMEON SHIMIN   *Listen, Rabbit!*
wash drawings and watercolor, 7½ × 10 inches

A painter with realism makes a book of exquisite
beauty in soft, gentle color that shimmers with enchantment. Always a storyteller, he steps inside a
child's mind, and with his love of nature presents the
rabbit world for a child to venture in. Shimin varies
his compositions with changing scenes that generate
excitement and wonder. The strength of his painting
lies in his sound draftsmanship, and one has only to
look at *One Small Blue Bead* to know this.

LEO LIONNI *Swimmy*,
watercolor, rubber stamp,
stencil, paper stamping,
9 × 10¾ inches

A child cannot own Swimmy or love Swimmy
or fish for Swimmy because he is a symbol.
However this brilliant tour de force of collage
and color succeeds because Lionni makes this
symbol a hero in a world of adventures and
puzzles. It is far better to accept the fact that the
artist fuses cool, muted sea-color with technique
into meaningful painted fantasy rather than to
list and explain his methods like a chemical
analysis.

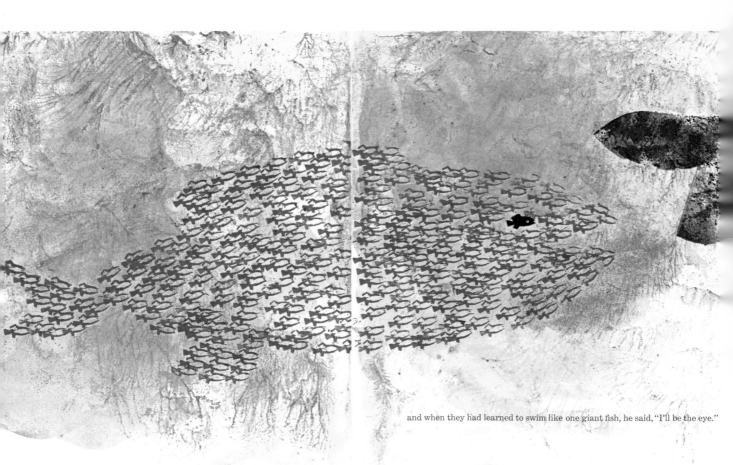

and when they had learned to swim like one giant fish, he said, "I'll be the eye."

MAURICE SENDAK
Mr. Rabbit and the Lovely Present,
watercolor, 7¾ × 6⅝ inches

This interplay between author and artist has true collaboration. Charlotte Zolotow does not describe scene or character. Maurice Sendak, completely absorbed, interprets the tale in luminescent watercolors that invite one to step along the woodland paths with Mr. Rabbit and the little girl. His contribution carries out the fantasy in the only way Charlotte Zolotow could have wished.

LEONARD WEISGARD   *The New Wizard of Oz*, line and watercolor, 5½ × 8¼ inches

When Leonard Weisgard paints, he works in glorious, sunny colors and silky textures to achieve solidarity and depth distinct from his line drawing. Here the tissue-thin poppies sway with the breeze and spread their deadly scent as they frame and entwine in the action. Weisgard can sublimate his own talent and retain the original, lovable characterizations as he interprets this classic and as he did *Alice's Adventures in Wonderland*.

LYND WARD *The Biggest Bear*, wash drawing, 7⅝ × 10½ inches

A story filled with pictures depicting an era of rural America is drawn with dignity by an artist who also has the eye of a naturalist. The young boy watches the bear cub grow into a majestic animal. Its friendly and tender relationship with the boy is conveyed with a fondness and personal involvement that a child can identify with. The artist's use of the one-tone sepia is as rich in value as if he had worked in complete color.

JEROME SNYDER
One Day in Aztec Mexico,
line drawings, 6¾ × 9 inches

This scene did happen in an Aztec child-hood. Pause a moment and stare at it; the men appear to spin around the flying pole in an amazing feat. Jerome Snyder, who assumes that children in any historical period are lively and playful, expresses mischievousness with authenticity and agility.

"My favorite festival of all the e
Tititl," says your brother. "And if the b
be his favorite, too. Oh, what a happ
have! We will pretend to weep to mak
will be a sacrifice and a feast, and the
be this: all the boys will stuff bags ful
them under their cloaks. Then whenev
lady or a girl, we will say, 'Here is a bag
give her a good smack with our bags, an
we will laugh and run!"

30

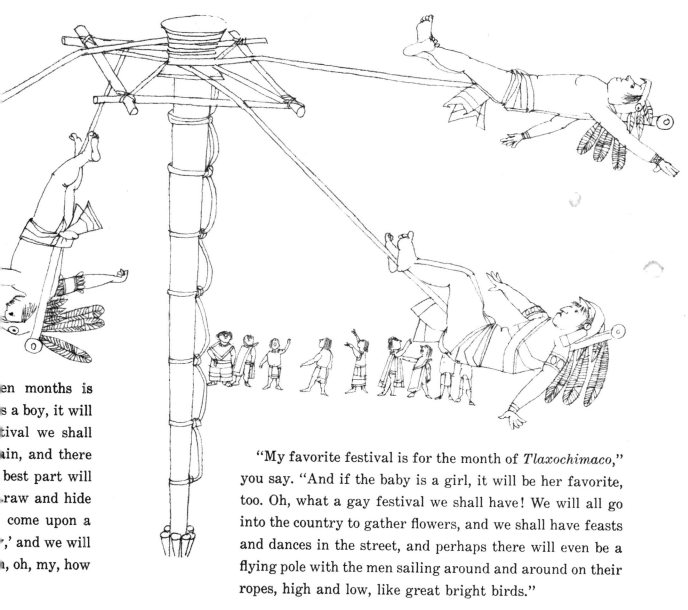

en months is
s a boy, it will
tival we shall
in, and there
best part will
raw and hide
come upon a
,' and we will
, oh, my, how

"My favorite festival is for the month of *Tlaxochimaco*," you say. "And if the baby is a girl, it will be her favorite, too. Oh, what a gay festival we shall have! We will all go into the country to gather flowers, and we shall have feasts and dances in the street, and perhaps there will even be a flying pole with the men sailing around and around on their ropes, high and low, like great bright birds."

31

GARTH WILLIAMS
Charlotte's Web
line drawings, 5⅜ × 8 inches

With reading books as compared to picture books, Garth Williams has a lovable, unaffected way of drawing pictures. His warm, almost human animals with their amazing facial expressions are inseparable from the story. Charlotte the spider and Wilbur the pig join the ranks of memorable artists' characters in children's literature along with Tenniel's Alice, Ernest Shepard's Mr. Mole, A. B. Frost's Brer Rabbit, and Mr. Williams' Stuart Little the mouse.

Poetic and Personal

ADRIENNE ADAMS

JACQUELINE AYER

MARVIN BILECK

BARBARA COONEY

MARGUERITE DE ANGELI

IRENE HAAS

DAHLOV IPCAR

BENI MONTRESOR

LEONA PIERCE

ALICE AND MARTIN PROVENSEN

SUSANNE SUBA

LEONARD WEISGARD

The wedding day arrived. The mole was already there to fetch Thumbelina. She would have to live with him deep down under the earth and never come out into the warm sunshine, for he didn't care for that.

ADRIENNE ADAMS *Thumbelina*, wash drawing in two-color and watercolor, 8 × 10 inches

A magnificent draftsman and a delicate colorist, the artist sustains an exquisite, ethereal quality throughout. Against backdrops of scenic beauty and meticulously furnished interiors are set her doll-like characters and silken animals for children to imagine the action that will take place. Adrienne Adams is gentle and sentimental.

Nu Dang's kite was the boldest and the bravest of them all.
It ran swiftly with the wind
and chased the birds that flew around the sun.
Nu Dang was the happiest boy in the grassy field.
He was the happiest boy in Siam.
He was the happiest boy in the world.
Nu Dang was *just* that happy.

And what beautiful and brave kites they were!
Kites that were birds,
kites that were snakes,
kites that were fish,
kites that were demons and gods.
The wind pulled them all high up into the sky.

JACQUELINE AYER *Nu Dang and His Kite*, line in color separation, 9⅞ × 7¾ inches

Here is a panoramic experience. Lucidly drawn in black line and with flat color freshly overlaid as in wallpaper designs, the settings are like an oriental bazaar where something unexpected is happening in every niche. One feels as if one had traveled to Thailand and followed the wistful Nu Dang on his jaunts and explorations. Jacqueline Ayer does not portray Nu Dang as a hero to identify with emotionally.

MARVIN BILECK *Nobody's Birthday*, line in color separation, 6⅝ × 8¼ inches

Inspired by the author's whimsy, Marvin Bileck lets his imagination run on and on with all the decorations and festivity of the birthday theme and creates the

When he opened his eyes, there was the Birthday that belonged to him. The Old Man was surprised and pleased and the children were pleased too. Now it was somebody's Birthday; they could play with the balloons and put on the party hats and snap the paper snappers.

feeling of drawings made of lace, tissue paper, and sugar frosting in captivating detail. He builds scene upon scene of surprise, activity, and excitement with real children taking part, and this outcome in fantasy is like a nostalgic burst from a party snapper.

"Hurry and open all your presents," they said to the Old Man, as they stood first on one foot and then on the other because they were so excited. He unwrapped and unwrapped the tissue paper and untied the colored ribbons.

BARBARA COONEY *A White Heron*, wash drawings in color separation, 6½ × 9¼ inches

A collection of landscapes, the paintings capture with beauty and intensity of detail the quiet setting for this poetic tale. Page by page the many moods of nature in Maine unfold, and the reader walks fearless and exploring through the woods to the end of the story. While the characterization has a resemblance to folk art, there is an impression of unbounded color by skillful use of a three-color palette.

MARGUERITE DE ANGELI *The Goose Girl*, line and watercolor, 8¼ × 11 inches

There is warmth and joy to these romantic scenes done softly in pencil and in color. The artist's compositions have a graceful flow as if she were telling the children a story while sketching the pictures and bringing her characters and animals to life, mainly in historical settings.

80

playing tag

or playing catch

or games

or digging in the sand

IRENE HAAS
A Little House of Your Own,
line drawings, 4½ × 9 inches

Irene Haas knows what children like to
do in their private world, and illustrates
their delights and quandaries in fine line.
Her pictures include little objects that
give the impression children have actually
carried and used them every day. The
scenery and settings to stories exactly
fit an author's descriptions as in her
illuminated paintings from *Tatsinda*
and *Zeee!*

DAHLOV IPCAR *Wild and Tame Animals,*
line in color separation, 10⅝ × 8 inches

A picture book can be an art object as in this one with its lively rhythm of
composition, patterns of color, and unusual contrasts in subject matter. Little

Elephants work in India clearing forests of trees and moving logs and lumber
to help build houses.

children will delight in finding and identifying numerous animals not in a story but rather in a picture-dictionary where Dahlov Ipcar has the animals dutifully and genuinely performing in their native habitats. The artist is versatile in drawing both wild and tame animals outdoors and in.

Blowing and puffing, the Wind pushed the pigeon across the entire city of Venice, but no one saw it because all around floated the clouds of dust raised by the Wind.

At twilight they arrived at the great palace of the Witches of the Grand Canal. The Wind was trembling with fear.

"Ch-child," he stammered, "now tell me how we are to get in."

The little boy crawled out of the pigeon and turned the handle of the palace door. The door creaked open. The witches had forgotten to lock it!

He got back into the pigeon, and the Wind began to blow again . . . and then the pigeon slipped inside the great palace of the Witches of the Grand Canal.

BENI MONTRESOR *The Witches of Venice,* line drawings, 9¼ × 11 inches

As an artist and a stage designer, Beni Montresor creates for each moment of the story a different and glorious set in a pantomime of fairyland, and tenderly puts his characters in the foreground. The bold black drawings with their intricate decorations and repetitive patterns of stone, water, and gardens, dazzle as they face pages of brilliant red type and give the impression that this book is in many colors.

I look up to the sun
and I want to say, "Thank you, sun,
for the shadow game."
But the sun is so dazzling, the sun is so bright,
I just close my eyes.
Then I feel the sun warm on my face, and
I hold my face up to the sun
and it feels good.

LEONA PIERCE *Who Likes the Sun?* woodcuts in color separation, 6¾ × 10 inches

Leona Pierce catches the daring and agility of children at play in the sun, and her surprising perceptions and strong color make the book a treasure. Examine the vitality in her handling of woodcuts simply executed and covering a wide range of subjects. In their realistic way they are as dynamic as the vivid abstractions by Paul Rand for *I Know a Lot of Things*.

JULIUS CÆSAR   ACT III, SCENE II

SECOND CITIZEN. Peace! Let us hear what Antony can
    say.
ANTONY. You gentle Romans—
CITIZENS.   Peace, ho! Let us hear him.
ANTONY. Friends, Romans, countrymen, lend me your
    ears;
  I come to bury Cæsar, not to praise him.
  The evil that men do lives after them;
  The good is oft interred with their bones:
  So let it be with Cæsar. The noble Brutus
  Hath told you Cæsar was ambitious.
  If it were so, it was a grievous fault,
  And grievously hath Cæsar answered it.
  Here, under leave of Brutus and the rest—
  For Brutus is an honourable man;
  So are they all, all honourable men—
  Come I to speak in Cæsar's funeral.
  He was my friend, faithful and just to me—
  But Brutus says he was ambitious;
  And Brutus is an honourable man.

He hath brought many captives home to Rome,
Whose ransoms did the general coffers fill.
Did this in Cæsar seem ambitious?
When that the poor have cried, Cæsar hath wept;
Ambition should be made of sterner stuff.
Yet Brutus says he was ambitious;
And Brutus is an honourable man.
You all did see that on the Lupercal
I thrice presented him a kingly crown,
Which he did thrice refuse. Was this ambition?
Yet Brutus says he was ambitious;
And, sure, he is an honourable man.
I speak not to disprove what Brutus spoke,
But here I am to speak what I do know.
You all did love him once, not without cause.
What cause withholds you then, to mourn for him?
O judgement! thou art fled to brutish beasts,
And men have lost their reason. Bear with me,
My heart is in the coffin there with Cæsar,
And I must pause till it come back to me.

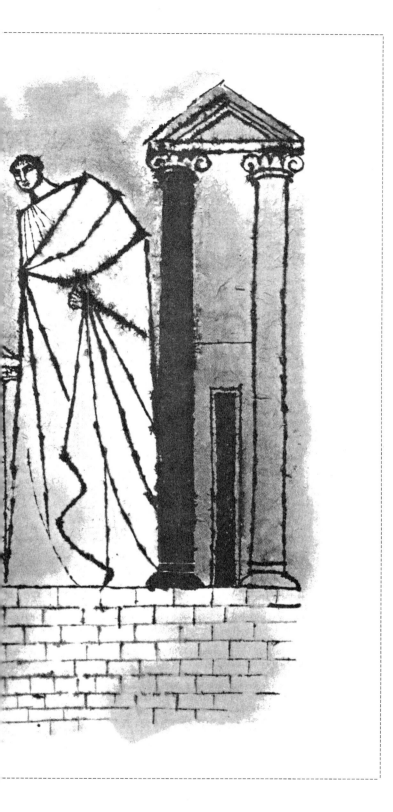

ALICE AND MARTIN PROVENSEN
Shakespeare Ten Great Plays,
line drawings and watercolor,
8¼ × 11 inches

In their fanciful invitation to Shakespeare, these witty and excellent stylists
convey the essence of live theatre on a
subtly lit stage. The staccato line heightens
this dramatic moment, classic in content and evocative in interpretation,
where the characters actually seem on
the verge of moving as a crowd. While
color is used, the power lies in the black
and white line.

Old Lady Fry
Wore heels a mile high,
And when she walked by me
I thought I would die.

SUSANNE SUBA
A Rocket in My Pocket,
line drawings,
6 × 9¼ inches

Suba has keen observation of the humor of any situation, and draws her children and animals in their moments of laughter, perplexity, sadness, and play. The cat really runs the sewing machine; the little boy laughs to himself. Because Suba uses white space as freely as she does her pen, these two unrelated pages complement each other spiritedly with just a suggestion of detail and scenery.

Oh, the funniest thing I've ever seen
Was a tomcat sewing on a sewing machine.
Oh, the sewing machine got running too slow,
And it took seven stitches in the tomcat's toe.

[7]

LEONARD WEISGARD   *The Secret River*, line in color separation, 5⅞ × 8 inches

What seems at a glance a tranquil scene is an illustration that is enchantingly appropriate. Leonard Weisgard brings forth the magic of experiences through a child's eyes, and introduces everything essential to the moment. Calpurnia is confiding in her dog beside a big tree outside the little house where she lives. Because the entire page is sepia-colored except for white highlights on the roof, tree bark, dress, and dog, one senses immediately Calpurnia is a Negro, and from the foliage that the setting is in the rural south.

Imaginary

JOAN WALSH ANGLUND
ANDRÉ FRANÇOIS
ANTONIO FRASCONI
MILTON GLASER
JOSEPH LOW
EDWARD SOREL
TOMI UNGERER

and some people have quite a few friends . . .

JOAN WALSH ANGLUND
A Friend Is Someone Who Likes You,
line and watercolor, 4⅛ × 6⅝ inches

Joan Walsh Anglund delights in small-scale vignettes of childhood experiences in which she recalls treasured moments and makes each one a complete picture story, romantic, idealized, and charming. The simply handled typography and the spacious *mise en pages* set off the friendly scenes. This is the first of a set of exquisite little books with children and gentle pets drawn in Joan Walsh Anglund's inimitable style.

MILTON GLASER *Cats and Bats and Things with Wings,*
line and wash in color separation, 9⅝ × 10 inches

Of interest is the fact that these drawings of fantasy were done first and, in time, the appropriate poetry appeared to accompany them. There is the impression of looking at Milton Glaser's private sketchbook and finding sixteen animal studies, witty, poignant, and expressively executed in interpretative color. However, the formal design that frames drawings and poems separately on facing white pages unifies the book for quiet exploration. Here, intent and fascinating, the crab slowly scuttles along the sand.

ANDRÉ FRANÇOIS
Roland, line in color separation,
8⅛ × 11¾ inches

The adventurous and daring André François
makes no concessions to the traditions of children's books in color or technique, although he
paints a merry story and at the same time an
absurd one in pictures. The hilarious way he
works is like an animated film with touches of
Matisse and Picasso. The typography leads one
right into the picture and on with the story, and
the more one looks, the more there is to find in
each scene done with mischief and tenderness.

The zebra bounded down a hilly stree
in the gutter and . . .

banana skin was lying

wind vento vent viento
wind   ven-toh   vahng   vee-én-toh

whale
hwayl

balena
bah-láy-nah

baleine
bah-len

ballena
bal-yáy-nah

ANTONIO FRASCONI *See and Say,*
woodcuts in color separation, 8¼ × 10⅜ inches

Antonio Frasconi has made the woodcut a graphic language. His simple, strong woodcuts in crayon colors are so vivid that children will relish pointing to them again and again. His choice of subjects shows a vast imagination and brings forth many new ideas to grasp. Adults will enjoy this book as a visual experience in the dynamics of design and typography by a master.

fishermen
fish-ur-men

pescatori
pess-kah-tóhr-ee

pêcheurs
peh-sheur

pescadores
pess-kah-dór-es

sea
see

mare
máh-ray

mer
mair

mar
mahr

anchor
ánk-or

ancora
ahn-kóh-rah

ancre
ahng-kr

ancia
áhn-klah

"Katherine, Kitty, **K**atydid —

What did she do? . . . She really did?

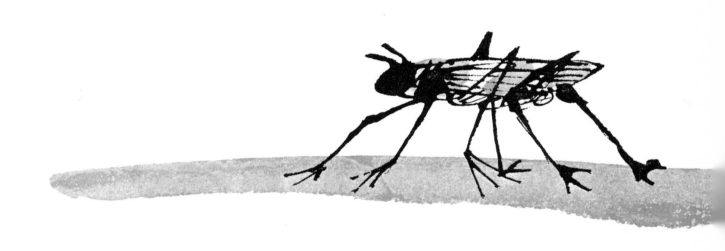

"Lovely little **L**adybug,

You must ask Eve to weave a rug.

JOSEPH LOW   *Adam's Book of Odd Creatures,*
wash drawings in color separation, 10 × 8⅜ inches

Joseph Low does beautiful drawings in fanciful books. Here, he lets one glimpse
into his private world where weird and humorous animals caper to graphic
perfection in fresh color, well-set type, spontaneity of pace, and ease of execution.
As an adult turns the pages, he could compare it to a visit in an art gallery.

He said, "You'll get your money's worth
And see the greatest show on earth."
The townsfolk came in macintoshes,
Rubber hats and high galoshes,
Weatherproof and watertight
For Mr. Flood's exploding kite.
It hovered there for all to see,
Its frame of purest T.N.T.
He soaked the string in kerosene
And started up the cloud machine.
Through smoky puffs the giant kite
Rose past the trees and out of sight.
The string was lit, the flame climbed high,
A huge explosion rocked the sky.

EDWARD SOREL
Gwendolyn and the Weathercock,
wash drawings and watercolor, 10 × 7 inches

Edward Sorel is a satirist with verve and pace who
can create a heroine, draw a story, and make a book
tout d'une pièce. He alternates panoramic landscapes in
a primitive style with lively animal and human close-
ups, all in electric color and with decorative detail.

So to use their treasure they gathered up all the lost,

unhappy, and abandoned children they could find.

TOMI UNGERER
The Three Robbers,
watercolor, 8¼ × 11⅜ inches

This is a fairy tale which is very much
alive. The subtleties of Tomi Ungerer's
point of view are for the adult's interest;
the humor, flamboyance, and wicked-
ness appeal to the child. A romanticist,
Ungerer dramatically repeats the patterns
of three in each episode and in the colorful silhouettes of his characters. When
mystery and terror change from bad to
good, the ominous black and blue are
replaced by red and then by a happy
ending in softer tones.

Collage and Abstraction

JOHN ALCORN

REMY CHARLIP

LEO LIONNI *(see color section)*

BRUNO MUNARI

CELESTINO PIATTI *(see color section)*

PAUL RAND

BILL SOKOL

WILLIAM WONDRISKA

Most books are just right for holding.

(Some are too heavy but none are too light.)
They can come in
all shapes and sizes.

Each piece of paper
in a book is two pages.
Like this.

There is a page on each side.
They are both necessary.

What is
not
finished on
one is

JOHN ALCORN *Books!* line in color separation, 4¾ × 7 inches

Books! is a delightful artist's rebus using printer's symbols and type as parts of the
illustration. Because of Alcorn's startling color combinations of pink, yellow,
and black in the various shapes and forms, the flat surfaces have that tempting
quality of a cutout book. The unrelated subject matter of the facing pages complement each other in design so that the total effect is attention-holding. The
artist succeeds in making the book a whole new object for child and adult.

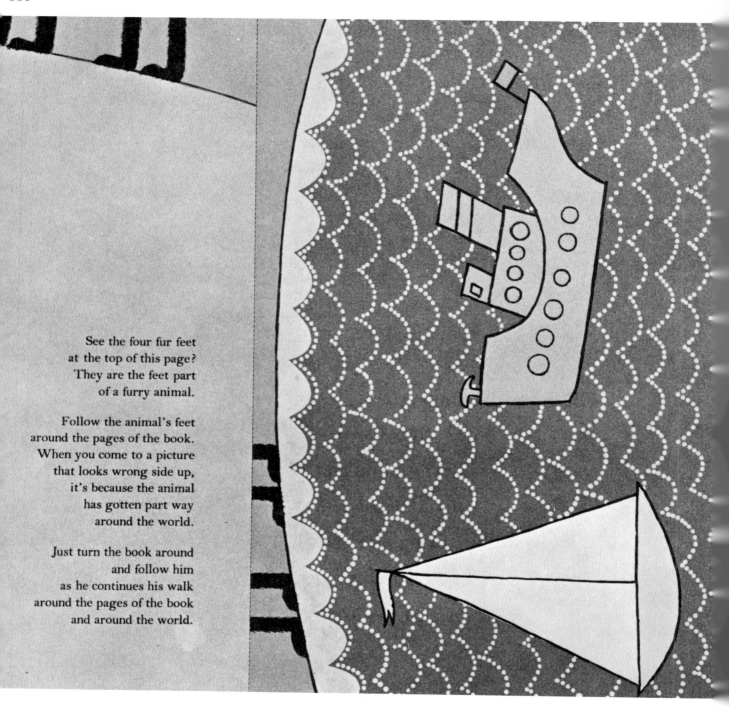

See the four fur feet
at the top of this page?
They are the feet part
of a furry animal.

Follow the animal's feet
around the pages of the book.
When you come to a picture
that looks wrong side up,
it's because the animal
has gotten part way
around the world.

Just turn the book around
and follow him
as he continues his walk
around the pages of the book
and around the world.

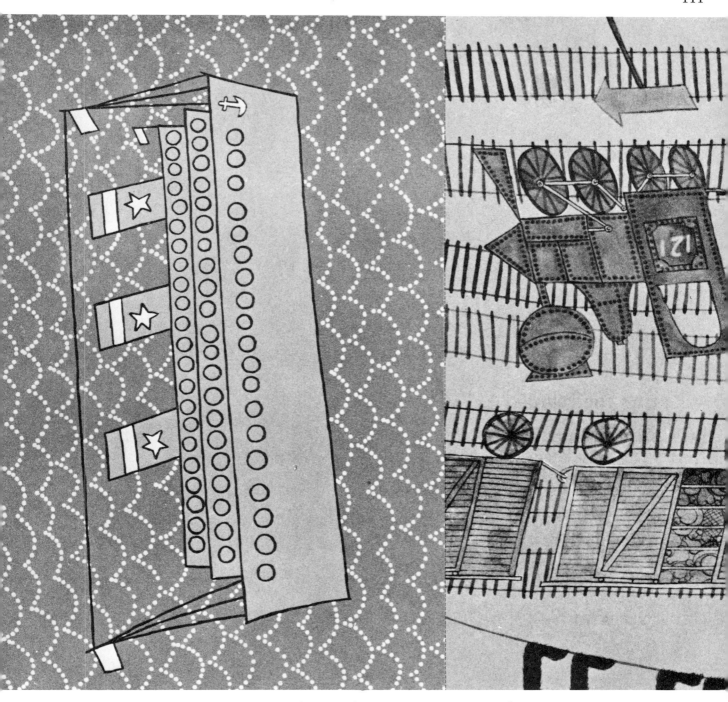

REMY CHARLIP *Four Fur Feet*, line in color separation, 6⅞ × 9⅞ inches

Because of his experience in juvenile theatre, Remy Charlip is aware of a child's delight in participation, and with his colorful, pristine drawings he is able to stir a child's imagination of play in a book. How cleverly he presents a fascinating fantasy and gives a new dimension to the physical properties of a book. He creates as a subject an abstraction of four fur feet. As these feet walk around the earth, so does the child follow them by turning the book to explore the animals and objects in fresh perspectives.

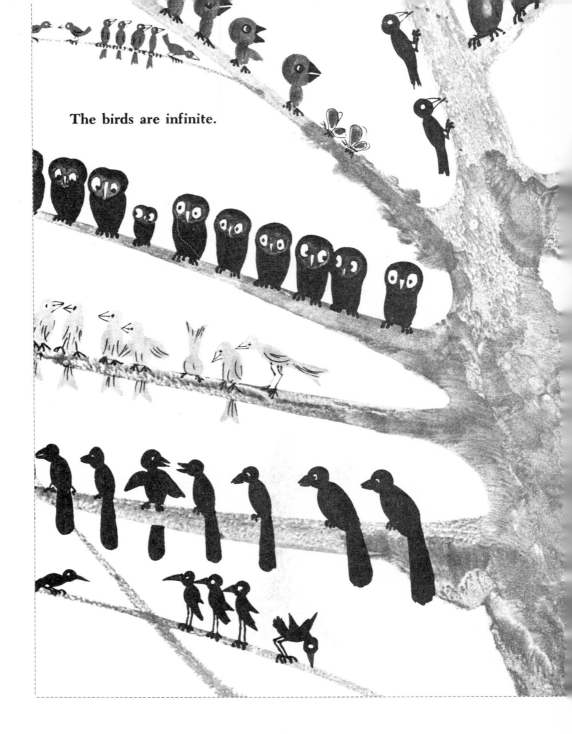

The birds are infinite.

BRUNO MUNARI *Bruno Munari's Zoo*, watercolor, 8½ × 11½ inches

A child enters his own zoo by following two butterflies through an imaginary opening in the wire fence on the binding, and how a child would like to do this! Once inside, the butterflies appear as a leitmotiv for the entire visit. Munari, expansive and spectacular, knows what a child hopes to find—animals groomed in dazzling colors and painted in action scenes and close-up portrait poses, even to a suggestion of their native landscapes. The animals' moods vary in fun, boredom, and wistfulness in this luscious picture book.

PAUL RAND   *I Know a Lot of Things*, line in color separation, 8⅜ × 10 inches

The artist's pleasure in doing this pseudo children's painting in a collage technique is contagious. Here is a puzzle expressed in simplest terms for the child to explore and to imagine that he is the hero of the situation. Note how Paul Rand is a master of form. Text, illustration, and color are so composed that the page could hang as a painting with its lyric, lilting quality. From a limited palette Paul Rand produces a kaleidoscopic effect of fresh clean color throughout the book.

or ride a big blue wave

across the sea.

You fly right out of the window.

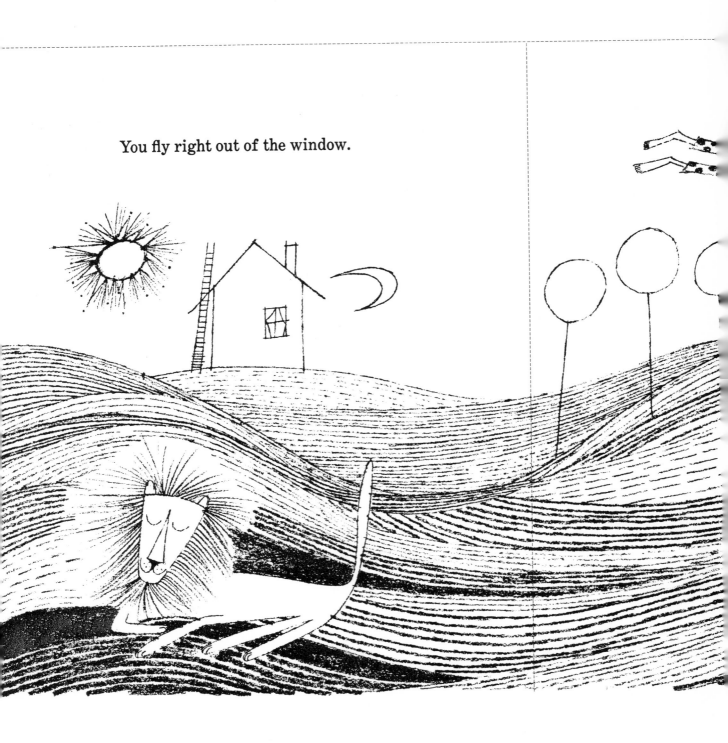

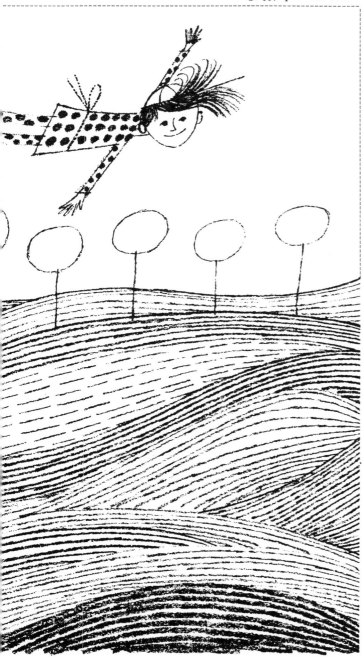

BILL SOKOL
A Child's Book of Dreams,
line in color separation, 6 × 7 inches

These drawings are whimsical graphics
of infinite design and humor. They carry
imagination and meaning without a
story and are, however, appropriate for
this prose-poem. Sokol uses the text as
part of the drawing and lets it give a
sense of balance to his compositions.

"I don't know," said Mr. Elephant. "Let's a

r. Giraffe. Which way to the Zoo, Mr. Giraffe?"

119

WILLIAM WONDRISKA   *Which Way to the Zoo?* line in color separation, 5 × 8 inches

William Wondriska designs a story in animation, and communicates by having the children count and identify more and more animals to enjoy this graphic work. The interplay of the black silhouettes against butcher paper makes for an exciting sensation of action across each page. There is no storytelling in the true sense, yet the whole effect is perfect and gives the child a feeling that he could take brown paper bags and make this book himself.

The Specialists

C. W. ANDERSON

ANTHONY RAVIELLI

SU ZAN NOGUCHI SWAIN

C. W. ANDERSON *C. W. Anderson's Complete Book of Horses and Horsemanship,*
stone lithographs, 7½ × 10 inches

C. W. Anderson considers each horse an animal with individual personality, and draws the equine character with understanding. His love of its conformation is evident in these knowledgeable lithographs. The artist maintains that a serious study can be pleasurable, and one could gaze for hours at his well-groomed horses, each with different markings and blazes and eyes limpid or alert, in head study or full stance.

The feminine look is not hard to see in these yearling fillies.

Now imagine a ball the size of a house.

To a fly st
ence it se
the fly sta
to the fly (

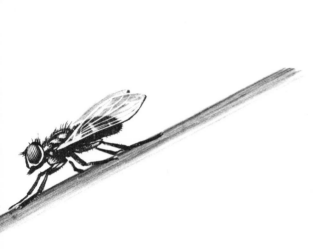

on this giant ball the tiny piece of the circumfer-
uld hardly seem to curve. And the part of the ball
would be such a tiny portion of the surface that
clever fly) it would seem to be flat.

17

ANTHONY RAVIELLI
The World Is Round,
watercolor, 7⅞ × 9⅞ inches

Ravielli finds the concepts of science as
fascinating as any work of fiction, and presents their many aspects in unusual and
imaginative relationships that are simple to
grasp and visually breathtaking. An expert
draftsman, he brings drama to an explana-
tion whether it is this fly walking in his
domain or a historic scene in actual color of
Columbus pondering the problems of
navigation.

SU ZAN NOGUCHI SWAIN
The Doubleday First Guide to Insects,
line and watercolor, 8¼ × 5⅜ inches

The purpose of any guidebook is to present a subject in all its rami-
fications for easy identification, and Su Zan Noguchi Swain achieves
this visually with her exquisite and authoritative paintings and delicate
drawings of insects. With the artist's touch she creates an orderly
classification that has graphic interest and invites one to study these
intriguing creatures.

LADY BEETLES

LADY BEETLE Some people call these beetles ladybugs or lady-
birds. They are very helpful to us. They eat lots of harmful aphids. There
are many kinds: red, orange, and yellow ones with black spots, and black
ones with red, orange, or yellow spots. They have names like Two-spot-
ted, Nine-spotted, and even Fifteen-spotted Lady Beetles. Lady beetle
eggs are laid on plants with aphids on them. They hatch into fierce larvae
which eat up the aphids. In winter great numbers of adults gather and
pass the winter in cracks in old logs and rocks and sometimes in houses.

JAPANESE BEETLE This beetle is very harmful. The larva eats
roots and the adults eat all parts of plants and trees. They have big
appetites and do much damage in a very short time.

JAPANESE BEETLE

26

BIBLIOGRAPHY

The Artist and the Book 1860–1960 in Western
Europe and the United States. Boston, 1961.

BLAND, DAVID. *A History of Book Illustration.*
Cleveland, 1958.

DELAFONS, ALLAN, ed. *The Penrose Annual.*
Volume fifty-four. New York, 1960. Rosner,
Charles. "Report on Poland," pp. 50–53.
Volume fifty-six. New York, 1962. Thomas,
David. "Children's Book Illustration in England,"
pp. 67–74. Bennett, Paul A. "American Children's
Books in a Changing World," pp. 75–81.

GILL, BOB and LEWIS, JOHN. *Illustration:*
Aspects and Directions. New York, 1964.

GREEN, ROGER LANCELYN. *Lewis Carroll.*
A Bodley Head Monograph. London, 1960.

LAMB, LYNTON. *Drawing for Illustration.*
London, 1962.

MCLEAN, RUARI. *Victorian Book Design and
Colour Printing.* New York, 1963.

MAHONY, BERTHA E.; LATIMER, LOUISE PAYSON;
FOLMSBEE, BEULAH, compilers. *Illustrators of
Children's Books 1744–1945.* Boston, 1947.

MILLER, BERTHA MAHONY and FIELD, ELINOR
WHITNEY, eds. *Caldecott Medal Books: 1938–1957.*
Horn Book Papers, Volume II. Boston, 1957.

PITZ, HENRY C. *Illustrating Children's Books.*
New York, 1963.
—— *Ink Drawing Techniques.* New York, 1957.

Quarto-Millenary. The First 250 Publications
and the First 25 Years 1929–1954. New York, 1959.

RYDER, JOHN. *Artists of a Certain Line.*
A Selection of Illustrators for Children's Books.
London, 1960.

SACHS, PAUL J. *Modern Prints and Drawings.*
New York, 1954.

VIGUERS, RUTH HILL; DALPHIN, MARCIA; MILLER,
BERTHA MAHONY, compilers. *Illustrators of
Children's Books 1946–1956.* Boston, 1958.

INDEX

An Index of Authors Mentioned on the Contents Page